Traditional Italian Recipes

7

© Copyright 2016: maria pacini fazzi editore
Tel. 0583 440188
mpf@pacinifazzi.it - www.pacinifazzi.it
imangiari.blogspot.it

ISBN 978-88-7246-526-4

Dreaming of the Tuscan Table

by
Carla Geri Camporesi

mp

maria pacini fazzi editore

Dreaming of the Tuscan table

Here we are again, revisiting the tradition, this time with a small gastronomic study of Tuscany. Tuscan loves to rediscover traditional recipes, enhancing them with the flavours of its land by adding distinctive fragrances: the frequent use of wild fennel, for instance, or of tarragon and wild greens picked in the fields.
The essential quality is that it's a simple cuisine, prepared for the most part with locally produced ingredients, whose best examples are the olives and its tasteful wine.

From the deep silence of its beautiful country side, with shady, cool, clay-covered hills, Tuscany offers a sweet, serene vision which induces meditation and the discovery of its infinite changing panoramas and the abundance of their very special flavours.

Together with the recipes found in my research, some Tuscan images captured by Paolo's pen also appear in this small volume.

Unless otherwise stated, all the recipes serve six people.

Sauces and hors d'oeuvres

Liver Canapés

10 oz. beef spleen, 4 chicken livers, 3 rabbit livers, 4 anchovy fillets, 1 tablespoon tomato paste, 2 tablespoons capers, parsley, long thin loaf of bread, 1 clove of garlic, salt and pepper, chilly pepper (optional), a cup of broth (or cube broth), extra virgin olive oil.

Warm two spoonfuls of oil with a whole clove of garlic. Extract the pulp from the spleen by scraping it with a knife so that the lean pulp meat comes out. Saute it in the oil. Using a different pan saute the chicken and the rabbit livers and when well browned chop them very finely and add to the beef spleen. Add the tomato paste diluted in half a cup of broth, stir the mixture until blended and cook for 10-15 minutes. Mince parsley, anchovies, capers, chilly pepper (if liked) and add to the mixture. Season with salt and pepper. Continue cooking for only a couple of minutes, otherwise the anchovies become bitter. Very quickly dip the toasted thin slices of bread in the broth and spread the sauce on top.

Crostini with olive paste

Special bread for crostini, 14 oz black olives, 1 lemon, 1 red or yellow pepper, extra virgin olive oil.

Make the paste by blending together the stoned black olives, a few tablespoons of oil, a few drops of lemon juice and a pinch of salt. Take a loaf of bread suitable for «crostini» – possibly a round one- and cut slices of an equal thickness, removing the crusts. Spread with the olive paste and add a few drops of oil and lemon juice as a seasoning. Decorate with little round pieces of red or yellow pepper.

Gamebirds Canapés

Small game bird giblets {thrush, blackbird, woodcock etc.), 2 tablespoons capers, 2 tablespoons butter, 1 small onion, 1 stock cube, 1 lemon, half a cup Vin Santo, nutmeg, salt, pepper, bread, one cup of homemade broth.

Wash giblets and chop them with a few capers. Gently soften one small finely sliced onion in the melted butter. Add giblets and broth cube and allow cooking. When nearly done, add the lemon juice, a pinch of nutmeg, salt and pepper to taste. Add as much Vin Santo as necessary to obtain a smooth, easily spreadable sauce. Cut some Tuscan bread into fairly thin slices, toast them on both sides, quickly dip them in a cup with some warm stock and then spread them with the giblet sauce.

Mushroom Canapés

7 oz. mushrooms (porcini (ceps) or ovoli), 1 clove garlic, half a small onion, a handful of parsley, 1 tablespoon capers in vinegar, 1 teaspoon butter, extra virgin olive oil, salt and pepper.

Clean mushrooms, avoiding washing them when possible. Chop garlic, onion, parsley and mushrooms very finely. Warm 2 spoonfuls oil and butter and gently brown the mushroom mixture. Continue cooking adding salt, pepper and small quantities of broth from time to time. When ready, add minced capers, more parsley and blend the mixture stirring gently and leave it to cool.

Prepare thin lightly toasted slices of bread and spread with the mushrooms sauce.

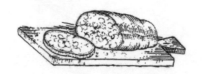

Olive toast

1 cup black pitted olives, 4 anchovies, 2 tablespoons capers squeeze out the vinegar, 1-2 cloves garlic, 2 tablespoon rum, 4 tablespoons olive oil, French baghette bread cut diagonally into slices.

Lay the bread out on a tray and toast in a 375 F degree oven until golden. Put the rest of the ingredients into a food processor and blend only briefly so that the anchovies, capers and garlic are finely chopped but not smooth; spread the cream on the toasts.

Green Sauce

There are many kinds of green sauces, that vary according to the ingredients added to the basic one, that is parsley. I prefer this variant that my mother used to prepare and is very easy to do.

A sprig of parsley, basil, mint, catmint, soft bread, vinegar, salt and extra virgin olive oil.

Chop a sprig of parsley finely with some basil, some leaves of mint and of catmint. Put these chopped herbs into a soup-boat with a nut-big piece of soft bread, previously dipped into vinegar and well squeezed.

Add some oil and a pinch of salt, stirring continuously in the same direction in order to blend the ingredients well.

Keep adding oil until you obtain a sauce of the right consistency.

Walnut Sauce

10 fresh shelled walnuts, 3/4 cloves garlic, a few basil leaves, a bunch of calamint, 2-3 table-spoons capers in vinegar, extra virgin olive oil, salt and pepper.

Peel the walnut kernels (if they are fresh it is easier) and chop with garlic, a few basil leaves and the calamint. Add the well drained capers from the vinegar. Mix everything with a wooden spoon, combine with olive oil as needed and add salt and pepper to taste. The sauce must be smooth and homogeneous.

When this sauce is used to season «ravioli with ricotta», as frequently occurs in Chianti, bear in mind to use capers in salt, which should be washed thoroughly and lightly dried before adding.

Panzanella

*4 slices of stale crusty Italian bread, 1 red on-
ion, 2 tomatoes, 1 cucumber, 1 stalk of celery, a
few basil leaves, extra virgin olive oil, vinegar,
salt and pepper.*

Soak the bread cut into thin slices in tepid water. Soak one very thinly sliced onion in cold
water with vinegar for at least an hour. Squeeze
well the bread slices, crumble them into a salad
bowl and add onion, tomatoes cut into pieces,
diced celery and cucumbers and basil. Stir well
everything, season with salt and pepper and add
oil and vinegar as needed.

Wanda Paola's meat sauce

4 oz lean veal, 3 oz lean pork, 4 oz mortadella (Bologna sausage), 1 cup milk, 1 tin of ready-prepared tomato sauce, 1 small tin of peeled tomatoes, onion, parsley, celery, carrot, basil, salt.

Cut up all the herbs very finely and fry lightly in plenty of olive oil over a very moderate flame. Add some stock if there is a risk of burning. Naturally, the stock can be prepared with a cube. You can also simply use hot water.

When the flavourings are well cooked, add the meat and the mortadella which have been carefully minced. Raise the heat and brown them well stirring with a wooden spoon. When everything is well blended, add the milk and reduce, again on a moderate flame. When the milk is all absorbed add the ready-prepared tomato sauce and the peeled tomatoes. Let it cook over a moderate flame until the oil comes out. Salt if necessary (be careful).

Maria Grazia's meat sauce

1/2 pound milk veal, 1 onion, 1 stock cube, spices, milk, salt and pepper, extra virgin olive oil, concentrate tomato, 1 oz butter

Put into a cold frying pan two generous table spoonfuls of olive oil. On top of the oil, form a small layer of large white onion, cut very finely. Immediately on top of this, using scissors, cut up 1/2 pound of very young tender veal which has been previously weighed and thinly sliced. Add the pepper, the crumbled stock cube and the spices (nutmeg, cinnamon) as much of each as you can pick up with three fingers.

Start to cook over a moderate heat, uncovered, and do not stir or touch it with spoon or ladle. When the onion has moistened, raise the heat slightly and brown the meat. At this stage, add 3 dessert spoonfuls of milk (better use a wooden spoon which is not so deep) and reduce. Now add a small piece of butter and reduce again.

Put two fingers high of concentrated tomato into a glass, dilute with water until the glass is full (if it's a small one), pour it all into the pan and further reduce. Taste for salt. When the water has evaporated the sauce is ready. The end result should be very pale in colour.

First courses

Pasta with parsley

1 scant pound shaped pasta (conchiglie), 2 1/2 oz parsley, a little basil, 1 clove garlic, salt, freshly milled pepper and extra virgin olive oil

Put on the stove a pan containing plenty of salted water, and as soon as it starts to boil, throw in the pasta and cook this until it is still crunchy (al dente). Meanwhile, chop the parsley and basil very finely, and brown the garlic in a glassful of oil in a frying pan. As soon as this is ready, add the pasta and the chopped parsley and basil. Transfer everything into a deep dish, season with pepper, mix it all together and serve immediately.

Bean Soup

2 oz bacon, 2 onions, 3-4 cloves garlic, 3 big carrots, 2 stalks of celery, 2 potatoes, 4-5 leaves fresh black cabbage, half a head savoy, 2 bunches Swiss-chard, a handful of parsley, a few sage leaves, rosemary, 2 1/2 cups beans («cannellini» or «borlotti»), extra virgin olive oil, salt and pepper, broth, stale crusty bread, 1 fresh onion.

Boil the beans in water (if dried soak them previously for a few hours) with a few drops of oil and a stem of rosemary; salt only when cooking time is nearly over. Gently brown, in a few spoonfuls of virgin olive oil, the sliced onions, cloves of garlic, and diced bacon. As soon as the onions become tender and transparent, add finely diced potatoes and allow to brown slightly. Add round-sliced carrots, chopped stalk of celery, striped black cabbage and savoy, a few sage leaves: dilute with some broth or lightly salted water and cook on a low heat for at least 2 hours. Remove rosemary from the beans, mash half of the beans and add their puree, the remaining whole beans and the cooking water to the vegetables. Lightly toast slices of bread, rub them with garlic, put into a tureen and sprinkle with oil, better if newly pressed. Add the hot soup and leave it to rest for a while before serving. Spread with fresh onion on top (keep the thinly sliced onion in cold water before using).

Longobard Soup

1/2 pound dry beans previously left to soak overnight in warm water, stale Tuscan bread, salt, pepper, extra virgin olive oil.

This is another way to prepare boiled beans, generally served as a first course. After boiling the beans, remove them from the pan with some of the cooking water and put them still piping hot directly into soup dishes, where you should have previously arranged slices of stale Tuscan bread, seasoned with oil, salt and abundant pepper.

Spelt and chick pea soup

7 oz spelt grains, 7 oz dried chick peas, 1 onion, 3-4 bay leaves, salt, peppercorns, olive oil

Clean off any impurities and then soak the chick peas in cold water for at least eight hours. Rinse them and put them on to cook over a low heat in a pan of water, adding a level tablespoonful of salt, a few peppercorns and the bay leaves. Cook them for about an hour and half. Chop the onion very finely and brown it in olive oil in a cooking pot, possibly an earthenware one. When the onion has turned colour, add the chick peas and the rinsed spelt, which has previously been cleaned and softened. See that the spelt and the chick peas are covered with enough water because they must simmer very slowly for another two hours. Stir continually during this time so as to make a thick soup. The longer it takes the better will be the end result. Serve lukewarm with a swirl of fresh olive oil. If the soup should thicken too much whilst cooking, add some hot water flavoured with a stock cube.

Pasta with artichokes

1 large onion, 4 artichokes, 3 oz butter, grated parmesan cheese, extra virgin olive oil, salt and pepper, 1 lemon, 1 pound penne or small rigatoni.

Wash the artichokes in plenty of water which has been added with lemon juice, then cut each one into at least 8 pieces. Cut the onion into small rounds and put everything together (i.e., artichokes, onion, oil, salt and pepper), Cook them for several minutes on a moderate heat, then add a glass of hot stock (made with a cube) and continue cooking for 30 minutes. Remove from the heat and add the butter.
Boil the pasta, drain, and season with the cheese and the artichoke sauce.

Mushroom Soup

1 pound of «porcini (ceps)» mushrooms, 2 cloves garlic, half an onion, extra virgin olive oil, calamint, 2 tablespoons tomato sauce, 1 chilly pepper, sheep's cheese, 2 cups water.

Cut the mushrooms into quite big pieces and slightly fry them in 2 spoonfuls of extra virgin olive oil, minced garlic and onion and a good quantity of calamint. Add a few drops of water, if necessary to maintain the mixture light. When the mushrooms have well absorbed the flavours, add the tomato sauce, the water, salt, pepper and, if liked, a few bits of chilly pepper. Leave the soup to simmer for a long time. Serve with plenty of grated sharp sheep's cheese.

Rice with liver, Florentine style

1/2 pound chicken liver, 1/2 pound rice, 1 on-ion, extra virgin olive oil, 1 cup tomato sauce, 1 glass cube broth, salt, 2 tablespoons butter, 4 tablespoons grated parmesan cheese

Fry lightly some chopped onion in oil. When it begins to wilt, add the needed quantity of rice, stirring it frequently with a wooden spoon so that it doesn't stick on the bottom.

Then pour in the tomato sauce, previously pre-pared and salted, and 1 glassful of broth, mix until the rice absorbs it, then leave to cook add-ing some more broth as soon as the rice gets dry.

Separately, lightly saute the chicken livers, cut into pieces, in a small quantities of butter. Afew minutes before the cooking time is over, add the livers to the rice, mix again, sprinkle the lot with grated parmesan cheese and serve.

Rice and lentil soup

8 oz lentils, 1 onion, 1 celery, 1 carrot, 1 cup to-mato sauce, salt, pepper, extra virgin olive oil, 10 oz rice

Boil the lentils, previously left to soak over-night in water and salt. Put in a pan, with two spoonfuls of extra virgin olive oil, a mixture of onion, celery and carrot, all finely chopped, and when it gets slightly golden add the lentils and the tomato sauce and allow them to flavour.

When the sauce is done, add some more water and cook the rice in it.

According to another recipe, instead of the above mentioned chopped vegetables you can fry garlic and rosemary lightly in oil: when the garlic is golden, remove it and the rosemary from the pan, add the lentils to flavour with a tomato sauce. Finally add some water, the rice and leave it to cook.

Rice in Chianti Wine

4 sausages, 4 onions, 4 cloves garlic, extra virgin olive oil, 1 glass red Chianti wine, broth, salt and pepper, 2 cups of long grain rice («Arborio» or «Carnaroli»), 4 oz grated sheep's cheese.

Lightly brown the minced onions and garlic in three spoonfuls of extra virgin olive oil. Add the sausages coarsely shredded. When they are lightly fried add the rice and allow to flavour briefly, then add a good cup of a best quality red Chianti wine. As the rice cooks, add hot broth in small amounts at a time. When it is nearly done, check the salt to taste and, if liked, add crushed whole peppercorns. Sprinkle with plenty of sharp sheep's cheese. Leave it to rest for one minute before serving.

Cabbage and bean soup
(Ribollita)

1 onion, 1 stalk of celery, 1 carrot, 4 tablespoons extra virgin olive oil, 1 pound cabbage, 2 potatoes, 4-5 zucchini, 1 cup tomato sauce, 2 bunches Swiss-chard (1 pound), 2 bunches red cabbage, 1/2 pound Tuscan beans, 1 pound stale Tuscan bread

This is surely one of the most famous Italian vegetable soups, whose two basic ingredients are typical of Tuscany, bread and red cabbage. Fry lightly, in olive oil, onion, celery, carrot, all finely chopped. When the onion wilts, add a cabbage coarsely shredded; when the cabbage gets tender, add 2 potatoes and 4 or 5 zucchini cut into cubes. As soon as these vegetables also become soft add 1 cup of tomato sauce, blend it with all the ingredients, then add 2 bunches of Swiss-chard, 2 of red cabbage and about 1/2 pound of Tuscan beans, previously boiled and mashed, (save some of them). Leave to cook slowly for at least 1 hour and a half.

About 30 minutes before the cooking time is over, add the saved whole beans, basil and thyme. In the meanwhile slice 1 pound of stale Tuscan bread into a soup tureen, pour in the piping hot soup and leave to rest until the following day.

Before serving put the soup again on the flame and leave it to simmer for 10 to 15 minutes.

Black rice, Florentine style

1 pound cuttlefish, 1 pound Swiss-chard, 1 pound rice, 1 onion, 1 glove garlic, extra virgin olive oil, salt, grated parmesan cheese (optional).

Clean the cuttlefish, laying aside the ink-sac, and cut them into pieces. Clean and wash the Swiss-chard removing the tougher leaves. Calculate 1 pound of Swiss-chard for 1 pound of rice and 1 pound of cuttlefish. Lightly fry some chopped onion and 1 crushed clove of garlic in oil until golden, then add the cuttlefish. As soon as the cuttlefish take on the characteristic reddish colour, add the Swiss-chard coarsely chopped. Mix, salt and leave to simmer for about 30 minutes. At this point add the rice, the ink and leave the rice to absorb the oil, then leave to cook adding tepid water. According to your taste, serve it with a sprinkling of grated parmesan cheese.

Pasta and chick peas

8 oz chickpeas, 1 clove garlic, rosemary, 2 fully ripe tomatoes, extra virgin olive oil, salt and pepper, 8 oz pasta.

Another extremely tasty and typically Tuscan dish, designed to enhance the fragrant flavour of fresh olive oil.

Chick peas, when dried, take rather a long time to prepare because they need to be soaked for at least 24 hours. Put the (previously soaked) chick peas, the peeled and chopped tomatoes, garlic, rosemary and oil into a pan containing $1 \frac{1}{2}$ and half litres of salted water and cook everything slowly on a low flame for a couple of hours. Now pass it all through a sieve and then put it back into the pan.

Season with salt and add the pasta (the most suitable is a small, short, straight kind).
Once on the plates, it would be a good idea to garnish it with a little raw olive oil.

Polenta with oil

12 oz maize meal, 1 litre water, salt, fresh pepper, extra virgin olive oil

For a good polenta it is best to use a copper cauldron. Failing this, use a large saucepan.

Boil the lightly salted water and gradually shake in the maize meal, letting it fall in one continuous shower. Cook it, stirring all the time with a wooden spoon. Control the consistency by adding either boiling water if it is too thick, or more maize meal if it is too thin.

When it has finished cooking (after about 30 minutes), use a wooden spatula, rinsed in cold water, to detach the polenta and turn it out onto a chopping board. Cut it into slices, using a colourless thread, season with freshly milled pepper and add extra virgin olive oil.

Tomato soup

(Pappa al pomodoro)

12 oz stale home made bread, 1 pound ripe to-matoes, 2 garlic cloves, 2 cups stock, basil, ex-tra virgin olive oil, salt and pepper

It is a classic dish of the cooking of the poor and no other humble dish can cope with it. The only ingredient that can't be replaced is the bread, which must be stale and home-made, the best would be the dark Tuscan bread.

Cut the garlic cloves in half and brown them in 2 tablespoons of oil. As soon as they start to change colour, add the peeled and diced toma-toes, plenty of basil, salt and pepper to taste. Cook it all for 15 minutes, and then add the boiling stock. When this has reached boiling point again, add the thinly sliced bread and con-tinue cooking for further 15 minutes, stirring frequently, and then remove from the buerner. After an hour, stir it all very energetically so that the bread completely disintegrates. Serve hot or lukewarm, adding a touch of good extra virgin olive oil and a few fresh basil leaves. No chees.

«Pappardelle» with hare sauce
(Pappardelle sulla lepre)

6 oz flesh of hare, 3 oz ham, 1 onion, 1 celery, 1 carrot, little parsley, 2 tablespoons butter, 2 tablespoons extra virgin olive oil, salt, pepper, tomato sauce, nutmeg, pappardelle (a kind of large noodles), grated parmesan cheese

Keep the entrails and the flesh of a hare. Chop the rather fat ham, onion, celery, carrot and little parsley, fry all of them in half butter and half oil. When the onion begins to wilt, add the meat, salt, pepper and leave it to flavour lightly.

Add abundant tomato sauce and leave it to thicken slowly, but take care that the sauce remains abundant. When the meat is done, remove it from the sauce and cut it finely with the half-moon, put it again into the sauce, adding some butter and a hint of nutmeg.

Cook the «pappardelle» in salted water.

Actually this delicious dish calls for home-made «pappardelle», cut from a not too thin sheet of dough.

Season them with the hare sauce and a sprinkling of grated parmesan cheese.

Spaghetti with clams

2 pounds clams, parsley, 1 garlic clove, 1 pound peeled tomatoes, extra virgin olive oil, hot chilly, salt and pepper

Wash the clams carefully in frequent changes of water to remove the sand. Put them without any seasoning in a frying-pan on the flame until they open (be careful to take them off the flame as soon as they are opened, as a protracted cooking should prove them tough).

When opened, remove them from the frying-pan and with a teaspoon take them out of the shell. So you can check if there is any sand left, in this case wash them again in tepid water.

Don't throw away the dark liquid remaining from the cooked clams, but tipping the pan, draw it off with a spoon, paying attention not to lift the sand laying down on the bottom.
Put some chopped parsley and garlic in frying oil; when the garlic gets golden, add some peeled tomatoes without seeds, the clams liquid and a tip of hot chili. Salt and leave the sauce to cook until thickened well.

At this point add the clams and leave the sauce to reach the boil once only, otherwise the clams become tough. Salt and pepper to taste
Separately cook the «spaghetti» until chewy, then season them with the above sauce and a sprinkling of chopped parsley.

Spaghetti with aubergines

Scant 1 pound spaghetti, 3 long-shaped auber-gines, 1 pound tomatoes, basil, 2 cloves garlic, salt, pepper and extra virgin olive oil.

Cut the aubergines into round slices, cover them with salt and leave for an hour to draw out the bitter flavour. Dry the slices and grill them. Meanwhile, make the sauce by lightly frying 2 cloves of garlic in two tablespoonfuls of oil, then adding the peeled tomatoes, salt and pepper. Cook these for 30 minutes. Boil the spaghetti in salted water and drain it when still only just firm. Add the spaghetti to the grilled aubergines and pour the sauce over them, plus a glassful of extra virgin olive oil.

Main courses

Roasted Duck

(Nana in porchetta)

A medium duck, wild fennel, 7 oz bacon, whole peppercorns, 2 cloves garlic, salt.

«Nana» is the name given to the duck in the Tuscan country-side.

Clean and wash the duck very well. Stuff it with a paste of diced bacon, salt and garlic. Rub the duck all over with crushed garlic and leave it to sit overnight. The morning after put it into the oven without any more seasoning and cook. Serve with roasted potatoes (potatoes cut into pieces and sauted in olive oil with 2 crushed cloves of garlic and 2 sage leaves, salt only when nearly done).

Veal Rib Roast

2 pounds of veal loin still with the bone, 3 table-spoons butter, 4 tablespoons extra virgin olive oil, rosemary leaves, salt and pepper, broth.

Separate the meat from the bone without re-moving it completely. Make quite a few holes between the meat and the bone and stuff with a mixture of butter, salt, pepper and rosemary leaves. Tie it up and put into the oven at 180 C (350 F). When it has slightly turned colour, add extra virgin olive oil and continue cooking, adding of warm stock in case the meat gets too dry.

Quails on toast

4 quails, 4 oz bacon, 1 onion, 1 carrot, 1 celery stalk, bay leaves, 1 clove of garlic, extra virgin olive oil, salt and pepper, 1 glass of white wine, 2/3 tablespoons broth, 1 oz butter, flour, Tuscan bread.

After having cleaned and passed the quail over a flame, wrap them in a very thin slice of dried salted bacon and place them in a pan with oil and some onion, carrot and celery (tied up in a bundle so that they don't melt in the sauce and you can remove them when the cooking time is over), some bay leaves, a clove of garlic, salt and pepper.

Fry the quails lightly, then add some dry white wine. When the cooking time is over, remove the bundle of vegetables, thin the gravy with a few tablespoons of broth, if necessary, and thicken it adding a knob of butter mixed with flour.

Separately toast and dip into broth some slices of Tuscan bread, arrange the quail on the bread, baste with the gravy and serve hot.

Duck «à l'orange»

1 duck, 3 oz bacon, 3-4 oranges, a few leaves of sage, a clove garlic, a bunch of calamint, dry white wine, Vin Santo, 1 tablespoon of flour, salt and pepper.

Clean the duck, remove the giblets and entrails, and pass it over a flame. Prepare the stuffing with chopped bacon, the rind of one orange (only the orange part), a few leaves of sage, crushed garlic, a bit of calamint. Stuff the duck, sew it up and grease it all around just enough not to stick to the pan and put it to cook. When it starts to brown pour white wine in and allow it to evaporate. In the meantime prepare a mixture by chopping the orange part of another orange rind together with the giblets and the heart kept aside, the juice of an orange and a bit of salt. Add to the pan where the duck is cooking, after removing any excess of fat.

Complete cooking adding small quantities of broth. Allow the sauce to reduce, take the pan off the flame and cut the duck into serving pieces. Pass the cooking juices through a sieve, add the juice of an orange, a spoonful of flour melted in a small quantity of Vin Santo. Add to the duck and put once more on the burner for a few minutes until hot again and let the flavours to be wholly absorbed. Arrange the pieces of duck on an oval serving tray, surrounded with slices of orange and basted with its gravy.

Stuffed Chicken Neck

1 chicken neck, 2 chicken giblets, parmesan cheese, 2 eggs, 1 bread roll, parsley, garlic, nutmeg, salt and pepper.

Clean the chicken neck very well and fill it with a stuffing made with the chopped giblets, the eggs, a good handful of grated Parmesan cheese, bread soaked in milk and well dried, chopped garlic and parsley, a bit of nutmeg, salt and scant of pepper. Sew up the opening to prevent the meat coming out. Add to the other ingredients as for preparing broth and allow to boil until done.

Siena Style Pheasant

1 pheasant (also chicken or guinea fowl can be used), 1 cup shelled sweet almonds, 1 cup prunes, 2 tablespoons shelled walnuts, 1 onion, 3 cloves garlic, 3 tablespoons butter, 1 lemon, 4 oi raw ham or bacon, juniper berries, cloves, ground nutmeg and cinnamon, 1 bay leaf, few leaves of sage, salt, pepper, chili pepper (optional), a slice of stale bread, a small cup of Grappa, a small cup of Vin Santo, Vemaccia white wine.

Clean the pheasant (or what has been chosen to cook) and cut into pieces. Saute a finely chopped onion in a little oil and very gently brown.
As soon as it fades add chopped ham or bacon, little butter, 1 bay leaf, sage, crushed juniper berries, a few cloves, a pinch of cinnamon and nutmeg. Add the pieces of the fowl and saute. When well browned, add the wine and a sauce which had been separately prepared (crumble in a pan a roasted slice of bread and lightly fry in butter together with the minced giblets, half a cup of Vin Santo and a bit of salt; when cooked, process in a blender until smooth). Add the juice of a lemon. Allow to cook for 15 minutes,

then add the chopped almonds, the minced walnuts and the stoned prunes previously soaked in white wine. Remove the bay leaf and continue cooking, adding some white wine if necessary. At the end, just before taking off the heat, pour the Grappa in and let it evaporate. Serve with grilled or roasted «polenta» slices.

Veal Chops with capers

6 veal chops, extra virgin olive oil, salt, pepper (optional), a cup of dry white wine, a handful of parsley, 2-3 tablespoons capers in vinegar, a few basil leaves, flour.

Coat the chops with flour. Warm a little oil in a skillet and add the chops, pour the wine over and let it evaporate. Mince together parsley, basil and capers. Arrange the chops onto a warmed serving tray, cover with the flavour mixture and leave them to rest for a few seconds. Serve with the accompaniment of potatoes cut into fairly small cubes and briefly brouned in oil with garlic and sage, then covered with tepid water and salted when nearly cooked (i.e. when water has completely evaporated).

Stewed rabbit with black olives

1 medium sized young rabbit, 1 cup black olives, 1 onion, 1 garlic clove, 1 carrot, 1 rib of celery, extra virgin olive oil, salt and pepper, dry white wine, vinegar, broth.

Remove the skin and the giblets from the rabbit, then cut it into medium pieces and wash well in water acidulated with vinegar to eliminate the wild taste it might keep. In a clay-pan lightly fry chopped onion and garlic in half a cup of oil. When softened, add carrots sliced in little rounds, minced celery, the pieces of rabbit and add salt and pepper to taste. When the rabbit begins turning brown, pour a cup of white wine in and let it evaporate. Add black olives and continue cooking, pouring hot broth any time it's necessary, to keep the rabbit tender.

The sauce can be used to season noodles. The rabbit is served hot on toasted slices of bread.

Pork chops with wild fennel

6 pork chops, 1 onion, 4 oz bacon, salt, pepper, extra virgin olive oil, fennel-seeds, 1 pound ripe fresh tomatoes, a cup of Chianti red wine, 1 cup green brined olives.

Cut the onion in thin slices, saute in little olive oil and add chopped bacon. When it starts to brown, add the chops and saute on both sides. Add a glass of red Chianti, salt and pepper and, when the wine has evaporated, add the tomatoes cut into pieces, a good quantity of wild fennel-seeds and olives. Allow to cook at a low heat until the sauce thickens.

Mixed meat soup
(La scottiglia)

1 pound chicken, 1 pound duck, 1 pound pigeon, 1 pound rabbit, 1 pound lamb, 1 pound veal or beef lean meat (quantities and qualities depend on available meat and personal taste), 2 onions, 2 cloves garlic, 1 rib of celery, 2 carrots, a few basil leaves, half a chili pepper, 2 pounds tomato puree, a cup of red wine, half a cup extra virgin olive oil, salt and pepper, bread.

Gently brown in a quite large pan the chopped onion and garlic with half a cup of oil. While they are frying, add sliced carrots, celery, basil, half the chili pepper and moisten with a few drops of water to prevent sticking to the pan. Prepare the different meats cut into fairly small and well cleaned pieces (fowls should be passed over a flame before cutting).

When the vegetables are well softened, add the meat, salt and pepper to taste and allow to brown for a while. Pour a cup of Chianti red wine in, let it evaporate, then pour the fresh tomato puree. Continue cooking until the meat separates from the bones. In case the meat gets too dry while cooking, add a few ladlefuls of warm broth. Serve on top of toasted slices of bread rubbed with garlic.

Fricassea

1 pound meat (chicken, veal, pork, lamb at one's choice), 4 oz butter, 1 tablespoon flour, 1 carrot, 1 stick celery, 1 onion, a little parsley, 2 eggs, 1 lemon, salt and pepper to taste, 4 oz fresh mushrooms

This recipe suits well with several kinds of meat: veal, chicken, lamb.

Put 2 oz of butter into a deep pan, when it has melted, add 1 heaped tablespoon of flour which has to melt and get golden in the butter, but take care that it doesn't brown. Then add 1/4 of hot water, a bundle of vegetables – carrot, celery, onion, parsley – tied up so that they don't melt in the sauce, 2 oz of butter and the meat. Whatever meat is used, it must be cut into pieces.

Add salt and white pepper, put a lid on and leave to cook gently for about 1 hour and a half. When done, whisk some egg yolks (according to the quantity of meat and calculating 1 egg for 3 people) with some lemon juice. Then pour this mixture onto the meat, keeping the pan on a corner of the flame and taking care that it doesn't reach the boil, as the sauce should prove creamy.

To get a tastier dish, when the meat is half done, add 4 oz of dried or fresh mushrooms cut into strips.

Florentine style Braised beef
(Stracotto alla fiorentina)

2 pounds of beef, extra virgin olive oil, 4 oz bacon, tomato sauce, salt, a pinch of spices, 4 oz dried mushrooms

Take a nice piece of beef cut from the rump and put it on the flame in a pan with oil and chopped onion, celery, carrot and the bacon cut into cubes. Leave all side of the beef get golden, then add some tomato sauce previously prepared, a pinch of salt, a hint of spices, and allow to cook slowly for a couple of hours, adding some tepid water from time to time. After the first hour of cooking time, you can add some dried mushrooms, previously softened in water and chopped.

Florentine style Pork liver

1 pound pork liver in a single piece, 1/2 pound pork net, salt, pepper, 1 clove garlic (optional), bay leaves, extra virgin olive oil

After having cleaned the liver and removed all the tough parts, cut it into cubes. The pork net has to be kept in tepid water to soften. Stretch the net out on the working surface and cut many square-like pieces from it, in which you will wrap the liver pieces.

Prepare a mixture of pepper, salt, chopped bay leaves (you can add also a crushed clove of garlic, but in my opinion the dish will prove too heavy in this case), and dip the liver pieces, so that they will be coated with that mixture. Then wrap each liver piece in a net square and close it with a toothpick.

Place the livers on a baking-pan greased with oil and leave them to fry with a lid on until nice and golden.

Galantine of Chicken or Capon

Capon or chicken weighing approx. 3 pounds, 1/2 pound milk veal, 1/2 pound lean pork, 1/2 pound chicken breast, 4 oz bacon, oz raw ham, 2 oz salted tongue, 1 oz truffles (also black ones), 2 oz shelled pistachio nuts, 1 egg, 1 bread roll, salt.

Bone the chicken or capon (or have it boned) and spread it out on a board. Salt lightly.
Prepare a stuffing. Roughly mince the various meats, the tongue, ham and bacon and mix these all together. Soften the bread in hot stock, shell the pistachio nuts in hot water, cut the truffles into fairly small cubes and add these ingredients to the mixture, plus the egg and a very little salt. Spread the filling over the prepared chicken or capon, reassemble the bird and sew it together. Also tie it up with special cooking thread suitable for use with roasts.
Wrap it in a very clean white cloth and boil in water for two and a half hours. Once cooked, remove the cloth, wash this, and then re-wrap the chicken or capon. Put a heavy weight on top of the bird to give it a flat shape and leave until the following day. It can be served with or without aspic jelly, cut into thin slices, either as a main dish or an in between course.

Cuttlefish in chard sauce
(Seppie in zimino)

2 pounds cuttlefish, 1 pound Swiss-chard, 2 cloves garlic, extra virgin olive oil, 1 glass dry white wine, 1 cup tomato sauce, salt, hot chilly, few parsley, 1 lemon

Wash some Swiss-chard, after removing the rib, and dip it into salted boiling water. Squeeze well and set it aside. Consider about 1 pound of Swiss-chard for 2 pounds of cuttlefish. Clean the cuttlefish well, cut the sac into rings and the tentacles into slices. Put 2 crushed cloves of garlic in a clay pan with oil and fry them until golden, then remove them. Add the cuttlefish, the Swiss-chard; 1 glassful of dry white wine. Salt and leave to fry for about 10 minutes, then add 1 glassful of tomato sauce, previously prepared, a bit of hot chili and 1 tablespoon of chopped parsley. Let cook for about 30 minutes. According to your taste, after removing the pan from the flame, you can also add some lemon juice.

Stuffed guinea fowl

1 guinea fowl, approx. 2 pounds, 4 oz chicken breast, 4 oz turkey breast, 4 oz lean pork, 4 oz cooked ham, 2 oz grated parmesan, 2 whole eggs, salt, pepper, a few sage leaves, extra virgin olive oil, 1/2 glass white wine, 4 oz bacon cut into long strips.

Bone a guinea fowl, leaving the claws and wings (it would be better to have this done directly by the butcher). To prepare the stuffing, mince together fairly finely the chicken and turkey breast, the pork and cooked ham. Add the parmesan, the eggs, a few sage leaves and salt and pepper in moderation. Stuff the fowl and sew up using a needle and thread. Wrap the bacon strips round fit and tie up to keep its shape.

Put the prepared fowl in a pan with three tablespoons of olive oil and a few sage leaves. Cook it slowly for about 15 minutes and add 1/2 glass of dry white wine. Continue cooking for about an hour and a quarter, then take the fowl off the heat and allow it to get cold. It's easier to carve when cold. Pour the warm cooking juices over it just before serving.

Dried codfish and chick peas

1 pound dried codfish already soaked, 3 1/2 oz tomato pulp, 1 onion, parsley, marjoram, 2 oz pine nuts, 2 oz raisins, salt, extra virgin olive oil, 7 oz chickpeas, 1 sprig of rosemary, 1 clove of garlic, extra virgin olive oil

Soak the chick peas for at least 24 hours, then boil them in lightly salted water containing a garlic clove, a sprig of rosemary and two tablespoons of oil. Drain. Dress with a good quantity extra virgin olive oil and freshly ground pepper. Keep warm and serve with the dried cod.

Put the previously soaked and skinned codfish into cold salted water, and boil for 15 minutes. Now drain the cod, bone it, and cut it into pieces. Put these in a pan, together with the roughly chopped onion and the tomato pulp, and cover with cold water. Boil it all slowly until the onion is cooked and the stock almost completely absorbed. Just before serving, scatter a pinch of chopped parsley and marjoram, the raisins and the pine nuts, and sprinkle with extra virgin olive oil.

Side dish

Mixed wild salad

The search for wild salads in the fields is a ritual reserved to the experienced. More varieties are found the better is the certainty of success when this extraordinary dish is brought to the table. Simple, tasty and «free».

Among the various salad grades, look for chicory, «radicchio», rocket, valerian, watercress. Carefully wash all of them, chop coarsely, add a few leaves of mint and season with first quality extra virgin olive oil and lemon juice or vinegar at will. Just a bit of salt.

Stewed pumpkin

2 pounds pumpkin (I mean the round pumpkin which grows in the kitchen gardens of the Tuscan country side) half cup extra virgin olive oil, 1 pound peeled tomatoes or 10 oz tomato puree, salt, pepper.

Cut pumpkin in medium pieces, flour and fry in hot oil to brown. Add tomatoes, salt to taste and pepper if desired. Cook at a moderate heat for about half an hour.

Onions cooked in foil

6 onions, extra virgin olive oil, salt, pepper

Wrap 6 fine onions (don't peel them) in an aluminium foil without any seasoning. Cook in a moderate oven for 3 hours. Just before serving unwrap them, remove the skin and season with extra virgin olive oil, vinegar, salt and pepper.

Stuffed Pumpkin Flowers

14 pumpkin flowers, a good half a cup ricotta, 4 oz bacon, 1 egg, 1 clove garlic, a handful of parsley, a pinch of nutmeg, Parmesan cheese, salt and pepper, extra virgin olive oil.

Chop garlic and parsley and mix with ricotta, an egg, 2 good spoonfuls Parmesan cheese, bacon cut in very small cubes, salt and pepper to taste.
Stir very well to obtain a creamy mixture. Wash pumpkin flowers, remove pistils and outer leaves. Stuff them with some tablespoons of the mixture, seal them well and fry in hot boiling oil, taking care the stuffing doesn't escape. Put them to drain on an absorbent paper and serve while hot.

They can be served as an appetizer or as an accompaniment to roasted meat or chicken.

Cardoons in tomato sauce

1 big cardoon, a tablespoon flour, extra virgin olive oil, salt, 1 cup tomato puree, basil, 1 clove garlic, half a small onion, 1 lemon.

Remove the outer leaves and keep only the inner white ribs. Scrape to eliminate fibres and cut into 3 inch pieces. Wash and boil in water acidulated with lemon juice. When done, coat them with flour, fry in hot boiling oil and drain on an absorbent paper.

In the meantime prepare a nice sauce: saute in olive oil the heart of an onion and garlic, both minced. Add a cup of tomato puree (better if home-made) and plenty of basil. Add the fried cardoons and allow them to flavour in the sauce for a while, before serving as an accompaniment or as a light entree.

Marinated zucchini or aubergines

1 pound small fresh zucchini (or aubergine) ,
vinegar, garlic, black peppercorns, 2 bay leaves,
salt and extra virgin olive oil.

ZUCCHINI: Cook the cleaned zucchini briefly in
hghtly salted water containing a little vinegar.
They must stay very firm - ten minutes should
be enough. Cut them into diagonal slices and
put them in a small salad bowl. Sprinkle with
chopped garlic, little grains of pepper and the
bay leaves. Cover the zucchini with extra virgin
olive oil and let them rest in the fridge for several days before serving them as a side dish for
boiled or roast meat.

AUBERGINE: Cut the aubergines into round slices, cover them with salt and leave for an hour
to draw out the bitter flavour. Dry the slices and
grill them. Sprinkle with chopped garlic, little
grains of pepper and the bay leaves. Cover the
aubergines with extra virgin olive oil and let
them rest in the fridge for several days before
serving them as a side dish for boiled or roast
meat.

Zucchini cooked as mushrooms

1 pound zucchini, 3 ripe tomatoes, 1 garlic clove, a bunch calamint, extra virgin olive oil, salt and pepper to taste.

The usual zucchini, only just harvested, light-green, small and firm. Cut into tiny stick-shaped pieces. Put these into a pan with a few small ripe tomatoes, a minced garlic clove and a small bunch of washed calamint. Sprinkle with olive oil, cover, and cook for ten minutes, adding a little salt. Pepper, if liked. Serve hot as an accompaniment to roast or boiled meat.

Baked Stuffed tomatoes

4 round ripe tomatoes (possibly of equal size), 1 good bunch of parsley, 1 tablespoon of capers (in salt or vinegar), breadcrumbs, salt, extra virgin olive oil, a little butter.

Cut the tomatoes in half, take out the seeds and put them with the cut side underneath to drain out the juice. Mince the parsley and the capers, adding the breadcrumbs, and make a paste of it with olive oil, seasoning it with a very little salt. Fill the tomatoes with this mixture, put them into a baking tin very lightly greased with oil and butter. Put a small flake of butter on each tomato half, and bake in a hot oven (390 F) for half an hour. They are also good cold.

Stuffed tomatoes

6 tomatoes (not too ripe), 10 oz tuna fish in oil, 2 oz parsley, 2 tbsp breadcrumbs, 1 fresh onion, 1 clove garlic, tarragon leaves, a few tablespoons mayonnaise, salt, pepper and extra virgin olive oil

Wash and dry the tomatoes, cut them in half horizontally and scour out the insides. Clean the parsley and chop it finely together with the onion, garlic clove and the tarragon leaves. Rub the tuna fish through a «passetout» sieve, add the chopped herbs, onion and garlic, and blend in a few spoonfuls of breadcrumbs, the mayonnaise, salt and pepper. Fill the tomato halves with this mixture and, before bringing them to the table, trickle a thin ribbon of olive oil over the top.

Valerian salad

14 oz valerian, 1 orange, 2 oz pine kernels, salt, parmesan cheese, balsamic vinegar and extra virgin olive oil

The valerian must be extremely fresh. Clean it thoroughly, leaf by leaf, put it into cold water for half an hour, then drain and dry it. Put the valerian in a tureen and add the sliced orange, the small thin slices of parmesan cheese, the pine nuts lightly saute in oil, the balsamic vinegar, the extra virgin olive oil and very little salt.

Dessert

Florentine «Schiacciata»

2 whole eggs, 7 tablespoons sugar, 10 level ta-
blespoons flour, 4 tablespoons olive oil, 7 table-
spoons milk, 1 orange, scant 1 tablespoon of
baking powder, icing sugar.

There are a thousand and one recipes for this
traditional Florentine sweet. Here is mine too.

Work together the eggs and sugar, thoroughly
add the oil, milk, grated rind of the orange, the
strained orange juice and flour, and mix again.
Then add the baking powder blending it well.

Butter a wide and shallow baking pan, put the
mixture into it and bake for 20-25 minutes at
200° C (390 F) When the «schiacciata» has
cooled to lukewarm, take it out of the pan and
sprinkle with a very thin layer of icing sugar.

Apple tart

5 apples peeled and cored, cut into thin slices, 12 oz sugar, 4 oz butter, 2 eggs, 1/2 glass milk, 2 level tablespoons flour, 1 teaspoon baking powder.

I have to say in advance that for me the amount of sugar given in the recipe is too much. However, I have to admit that the quantity indicated gives the tart a very special caramel flavour which is lost if less sugar is used. I suggest you to try out once the recipe as it stands and then possibly adjust it later according to your own taste. This recipe has quite an unusual history. The restaurant where the tart is offered is very possessive of the recipe and it was never possible to obtain.

One day we had invited a friend who is a very distinguished and popular Italian film actor and when he asked for the recipe they did not know how to refuse this. It is a simple recipe but it was not easy to imagine what the ingredients were. You will notice this immediately.

Proceed by slicing the five apples very thinly

(the quality is not important). Separately, blend the eggs, milk and sugar. Mix them together a bit, and then add the flour, melted butter, raising agent and the apples. Put it all in the buttered baking dish, and cook for one hour at 320-350 F. It does not matter much if it burns a little. Serve hot after letting it rest for some minutes.

I call it my jolly tart. Everyone likes it very much. I prepare it at the last minute and it never disappoints.

Bomboloni

1/2 pound peeled potatoes, 1/2 pound flour, 1 whole egg and 1 yolk, nut sized piece of butter, 3-4 tablespoons sugar, 1 lemon, 1 oz brewer's yeast, milk

Cut the potatoes into small pieces and either steam them, or if they are boiled, take them out of the water whilst they are still firm and have not absorbed any water. Put the butter and grated lemon rind into a bowl with the hot sieved potatoes. Add the separately beaten egg and egg yolk, the sugar and the flour. Finally, add the yeast dissolved in barely lukewarm milk. Mix everything well together, cover the bowl and put it in a warm place, away from draughts, but not in the oven.

After an hour the dough will have doubled in size. On the table prepare some cloths, folded double, because the bomboloni must stay warm, covered up, until ready to fry, and they will continue to rise. When the dough is divided up, the above amounts are sufficient for 20-30 discs, 6 cm. in diameter, using a glass to cut them out. Take them out from under the cloth one at a time and deep fry them in corn seed oil, in small quantities. Drain on absorbent kitchen paper and sprinkle with a little sugar.

N.B. If they are made when the weather is very hot, they can be put without the cloth, in a cool place. This slows down the rising process a little.

Rosemary bread

2 pounds flour, 2 oz brewer's yeast, 2 oz sugar, 1/2 glass extra virgin olive oil, 4 oz raisins, 2 tablespoons rosemary leaves, 1 egg.

Mix into dough 2 pounds of sieved white flour, 2 oz of brewer's yeast, tepid water and 2 oz of sugar. Leave it to rise in a tepid place until it doubles. Then put it on the rolling-board, add to it 1 glassful and a half of olive oil, 4 oz of. raisins and some tablespoons of rosemary leaves. Form many dome-shaped rolls, brush them over with beaten egg and make a cross on their surface with a pair of scissors.
Bake them in a hot oven and take them out when the surface gets a golden crust.

The «Panforte» of Siena

This is one of the many home-made «panforte» recipes that can be found in the Siena area. Here I have managed to eliminate the difficulties of the traditional recipe, too elaborate and whose ingredients are not always all available. The result is satisfactory indeed and the preparation can easily be made at home too.

1 1/4 cups shelled sweet almonds, 1 cup walnuts, 1/2 cup dried figs, 1/2 cup honey, 1/2 cup candied citron, 1/2 cup candied pumpkin, 1/2 cup candied orange, 1/2 cup shelled hazelnuts, 1 cup icing sugar, 1/2 cup sweet cocoa, 2 tablespoons ground cinnamon, 2 tablespoons of a mixture of cloves, white pepper, coriander and nutmeg, all ground, wafers to line the mould, butter.

Heat the almonds and walnuts in boiling water. Remove the peel, chop them and let them slightly dry in a lukewarm oven. Toast the hazelnuts in the oven and remove the peel rubbing them on the table with a cloth and coarsely chop them too. Finely dice the candied and the dried fruit and mix in a tureen. Dust with cocoa, add spices and half of the cinnamon and stir to blend. Separately, mix the honey with a scant cup of sugar in a small casserole with a concave bottom (the most suitable is the not tinned copper), stir with a wooden spatula until melted, then cook gently on a very low heat for 10 minutes. Take off heat, add the fruit and blend carefully. Now line a lightly buttered spring-pan with wafers, pour the mixture in and evenly spread the top, then bake in the oven at a moderate heat (160 F) for 30-40 minutes. When ready, let cool down and remove the cake from the mould. Sprinkle with the remaining sugar and cinnamon. Keep in a dry place wrapped in aluminium foil.

Chestnut Pancakes

1/2 pound chestnut flour, little salt, water, 4 oz sultanas, extra virgin olive oil.

The usual smooth batter made with chestnut flour, water, a little salt, sultanas previously softened in lukewarm water, grated orange or lemon peel according to taste and sometimes availability. To be fried, a spoonful at a time in hot olive oil. As they become slightly greasy, it is a good idea to drain them on absorbent kitchen paper.

Pine-nut tart
(Pinolata)

2 1/2 cups flour, 1 1/2 cups sugar, 4 eggs, 1/4 cup shelled pine-nuts, 2 spoonfuls butter, 1 lemon.

Whisk together well the egg yolks and sugar. Add less than 1 spoonful butter, melted in a Bain Marie, flour, pine-nuts and the stiffly-beaten egg whites. Butter a round baking-tin, 11 inch in diameter, pour the mixture in and bake at 350 F for about half an hour. It can be served soaked with Grand Marnier or other liqueur and stuffed with a very good custard.

Index

Sauces and hors d'oeuvres

Liver Canapes	9
Crostini with olive paste	10
GamebirdsCanapes	11
Mushroom Canapes	12
Olive toast	13
Green Sauce	14
Walnut Sauce	15
Panzanella	16
Wanda Paola's meat sauce	17
Maria Grazia's meat sauce	18

First courses

Longobard Soup	21
Bean Soup	22
Pasta with parsley	23
Spelt and chick peas	24
Pasta with artichokes	25
Mushroom Soup	26
Rice with liver, Florentine style	27
Rice and lentils soup	28
Rice in Chianti Wine	29
Black rice, Florentine style	30

Ribollita   31
Pasta and chick peas   33
Polenta with oil   34
Tomato soup   35
Pappardelle sulla lepre   36
Spaghetti with clams   37
Spaghetti with aubergines   38

Main courses

Roasted Duck   41
Veal Rib Roast   42
Quail on toast   43
Stuffed Chicken Neck   44
Duck «a l'orange»   44
Pheasant Siena Style   46
Veal Chops with capers   47
Stewed rabbit with black olives   48
Pork chops with wild fennel   49
Mix Meat Soup   50
Fricassea   51
Braised beef, Florentine style   52
Pork liver, Florentine style   53
Galantine of Chicken or Capon   54
Stuffed guinea fowl   55
Cattlefish in chard sauce   56
Dried codfish and chick peas   57

Side dish

Mixed wild salad   61
Stewed pumpkin   62
Onions cooked in foil   62
Stuffed Pumpkin Flowers   63
Cardoons in tomato sauce   64
Marinated zucchini or aubergines   65
Zucchini cooked as mushrooms   66
Baked Stuffed tomatoes   67
Stuffed tomatoes   68
Valerian salad   69

Dessert

Apple tart   73
Bomboloni   74
Rosemary bread   76
Schiacciata fiorentina   77
Chestnut Pancakes   78
The «Panforte» of Siena   79
Pin-nut tart   81

Traditional Italian Recipes

PUBLISHED PRICE € 4,50

Traditional Recipes of lucchesian farmers

Traditionelle Luccheser Gerichte

Carla Geri Camporesi
Cooking with olive oil

Carla Geri Camporesi
Traditional recipes from Florence

Carla Geri Camporesi
Siena und der Chianti

Sandra Lotti
A Taste of Tuscany

Carla Geri Camporesi
Dreaming of the Tuscan Table

Carla Geri Camporesi
The use of garlic in the Tuscan table

Barbara Golini
For love of chocolate

Luciano Mignolli
Farro. All Spelt Recipes

Carla Geri Camporesi - Barbara Golini
Curiosities and Delights of Tuscany

Finito di stampare nel mese di febbraio 2016
per conto di maria pacini fazzi editore